COAST PEOPLE
Life on the north east coast

Ian Forsyth

COAST PEOPLE
Life on the north east coast

For my daughter Rose, and the sandcastles you never had the chance to make.

www.ianforsythphotographer.com

First published 2015 by DB Publishing, an imprint of JMD Media Ltd,
Nottingham, United Kingdom.

ISBN 978-1-78091-507-4

Printed and bound by Copytech (UK) Ltd, Peterborough

Contents

Introduction

The great Magnum photographer Elliott Erwitt once said, "The whole point of taking photographs is that you don't have to explain things with words".

In Coast People Ian Forsyth takes heed of Erwitt and keeps explanatory captions to a minimum preferring to captivate the viewer with beautiful imagery as he takes us on a journey along 85 miles of the North East coast from South Gare at the mouth of the River Tees to the rocky drama of Flamborough Head in Yorkshire.

His 190 black and white photographs are uncomplicated, humorous and full of affection for the people who figure in them. Fishermen, surfers, dog walkers, picnickers, eccentrics, beachcombers, snoozers and those who head for the beach in all weathers simply to find peace and quiet adorn the pages.

Ian has travelled all over the globe serving in the military but his love for this particular stretch of coastline and its people shines through. However, this book is not just a collection of pretty pictures. North East fishing and its associated industries are in decline and communities are suffering badly in these austere times. Ian's determination to honestly chronicle everyday life in the area where he himself lives before it changes forever is in the best tradition of British documentary photography.

Tom Stoddart

Fisherman Gordon Brudenell digs for bait, South Gare, Teesside.

A fisherman from the Fisherman's Association, South Gare, Teesside.

Fisherman Colin Oliver in his fisherman's hut, South Gare, Teesside.

Fisherman James While in his fisherman's hut, South Gare, Teesside.

Fishing from the breakwater, South Gare, Teesside.

Surfers watch a winter swell, South Gare, Teesside.

Alison Wake feeds seabirds, South Gare, Teesside.

Fishermen enjoy the afternoon sun at Paddy's Hole, South Gare, Teesside.

A fisherman pulls a boat up a slipway, Paddy's Hole, South Gare, Teesside.

Lone fisherman, South Gare, Teesside.

A surfer rides a wave, South Gare, Teesside.

Laurel and Hardy, Redcar seafront, Cleveland.

Couple on a windswept beach, Majuba Beach, Redcar, Cleveland.

Woman wrapped in blanket, Redcar beach, Cleveland.

Boxing Day dip, Redcar, Cleveland.

Morning swim, Redcar beach, Cleveland.

Stranded seal, Redcar beach, Cleveland.

Mobility scooters, Redcar stray, Cleveland.

Offshore wind farm construction, Redcar, Cleveland.

Kite Surfer, Majuba beach, Redcar, Cleveland.

Fishing boat heads out, Redcar Beach, Cleveland.

Ray Preston from Coastwatch, Redcar, Cleveland.

Land yacht racer Ian Dibdin, Coatham sands, Redcar, Cleveland.

New Year's Day dip, Redcar, Cleveland.

Couple on the beach, Saltburn, Cleveland.

Backwash wave, Saltburn, Cleveland.

Upper Promenade, Saltburn, Cleveland.

Couple on the Victorian Pier, Saltburn, Cleveland.

Sitting on the sea wall, Saltburn, Cleveland.

Lower Promenade, Saltburn, Cleveland.

Eating chips in the bandstand, Saltburn, Cleveland.

Homeless man Mr Geebers, seafront, Saltburn, Cleveland.

Eating chips on a snowy day, Lower Promenade, Saltburn, Cleveland.

Crowded beach, Saltburn, Cleveland.

End of the pier, Saltburn, Cleveland.

Fishing boat returns, Saltburn, Cleveland.

Boxing Day Dip, Saltburn, Cleveland.

Young boy on the beach, Saltburn, Cleveland.

Horses riding out, Saltburn, Cleveland.

SALTBURN SURF SCHOOL AND HIRE

Nick Noble from Saltburn Surf School and Hire, Saltburn, Cleveland.

Tai Chi on the beach, Saltburn, Cleveland.

Lone man walks along the beach, Huntcliff, Saltburn, Cleveland.

Woman and dog sit on the pier, Saltburn, Cleveland.

Crew of the 'Ellen' load up, Saltburn, Cleveland.

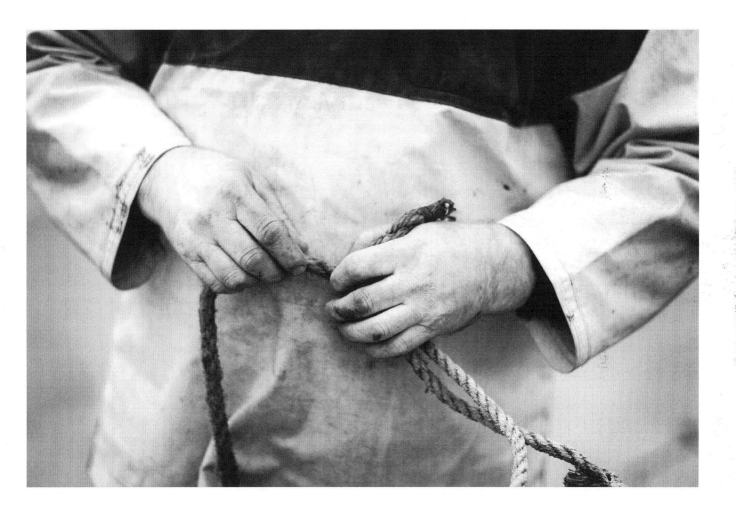

Fisherman's hands, Saltburn, Cleveland.

Collecting winkles from the reef, Huntcliff, Saltburn, Cleveland.

Collecting winkles from the reef, Huntcliff, Saltburn, Cleveland.

Surfers against Sewage beach clean, Saltburn, Cleveland.

Slack lining under the pier, Saltburn, Cleveland.

A man sleeps on a bench, Upper Promenade, Saltburn, Cleveland.

Dead porpoise washed onto the beach, Saltburn, Cleveland.

Graffiti on seawall, Saltburn, Cleveland.

A couple sit looking out to sea, Saltburn, Cleveland.

Sam Davis and 'Meg', Saltburn, Cleveland.

Metal detecting, Saltburn, Cleveland.

Beach fishing, Saltburn, Cleveland.

Stormy weather, Lower Promenade, Saltburn, Cleveland.

Kayak fishing, Saltburn, Cleveland.

Sandcastles, Saltburn, Cleveland.

A photographer waits for the right light, Saltburn, Cleveland.

Casting from the end of the pier, Saltburn, Cleveland.

Fish and chips, Lower Promenade, Saltburn, Cleveland.

Beach huts, Saltburn, Cleveland.

Rehearsing on the pier, Saltburn, Cleveland.

RNLI Lifeguard Nick Woodings, Saltburn, Cleveland.

Sheltering from the sea breeze, Saltburn, Cleveland.

Surfboard shaper Glenn Nary, Saltburn, Cleveland.

Surfer Karl Frampton, Saltburn, Cleveland.

Surfers sit under storm clouds, Saltburn, Cleveland.

The 'Senna' is launched, Saltburn, Cleveland.

Boxing Day dip, Saltburn, Cleveland.

Dean Dandy collects sea coal, Saltburn, Cleveland.

Dean Dandy collects sea coal, Saltburn, Cleveland.

Dawn surf session, Saltburn, Cleveland.

Surfer Tom Davis, Saltburn, Cleveland.

Misty beach, Saltburn, Cleveland.

Lone stand-up paddle boarder, Saltburn, Cleveland.

Foggy beach, Saltburn, Cleveland.

RNLI inshore boat practices, Saltburn, Cleveland.

Stand-up paddle boarder Simon Dunton, Saltburn, Cleveland.

Fisherman Tony Savage, Saltburn, Cleveland.

Fisherman Gary Hewitt, Saltburn, Cleveland.

Fisherman Bill Stocker, Saltburn, Cleveland.

Fisherman Denise Waring, Saltburn, Cleveland.

Artist Piers Browne, Saltburn, Cleveland.

Musician on pier, Saltburn, Cleveland.

The happy couple, Saltburn pier, Saltburn, Cleveland.

The water bottles, Saltburn, Cleveland.

Reading on the rocks, Saltburn, Cleveland.

Sitting on the seawall, Saltburn, Cleveland.

A fishing boat heads in after finishing for the day, Saltburn, Cleveland.

Beach barbecue, Saltburn, Cleveland.

Fishing at the river mouth, Saltburn, Cleveland.

Having a kick about, Saltburn, Cleveland.

Watching the waves, Saltburn, Cleveland.

RNLI beach lifeguards Elisha Doi and Evan Rogers, Saltburn, Cleveland.

Seating for restaurant customers only, Saltburn, Cleveland.

Saxophonist John McGough, Saltburn, Cleveland.

Sea kayakers, Saltburn, Cleveland.

Lower Promenade, Saltburn, Cleveland.

Sitting on the beach, Saltburn, Cleveland.

Dancer Zeta Hill rehearses, Saltburn, Cleveland.

Sea coaler, Saltburn, Cleveland.

Bonfire and firework night, Skinningrove, North Yorkshire.

Fishing boat, Skinningrove, North Yorkshire.

Standing on the dunes at sunset, Skinningrove, North Yorkshire.

Surfer Frazer Camfield, Staithes, North Yorkshire.

Surfer tucks into a barrel, Staithes, North Yorkshire.

Throwing a baited lobster pot back in at low tide, Staithes, North Yorkshire.

Looking out to sea from the cliffs, Staithes, North Yorkshire.

Walking through the town, Staithes, North Yorkshire.

A Lone fishing boat, Staithes, North Yorkshire.

Wine and weekend break, Staithes, North Yorkshire.

Afternoon stroll, Runswick Bay, North Yorkshire.

Sea swimmer, Sandsend, North Yorkshire.

Dodging the waves, Sandsend, North Yorkshire.

Fishing from Lythe car park, Sandsend, North Yorkshire.

Couple watch the waves crashing, Sandsend, North Yorkshire.

Spring tides, Sandsend, North Yorkshire.

Watching the waves break, Sandsend, North Yorkshire.

Stone balancing, Sandsend, North Yorkshire.

Walking along the pier, Whitby, North Yorkshire.

Clara's Cafe, Whitby, North Yorkshire.

Scooter Rally, Whitby, North Yorkshire.

Goth weekend, Whitby pier, North Yorkshire.

Captain Cook statue, West Cliff, Whitby, North Yorkshire.

Bailiff Lol Hodgson carries out the Penny Hedge tradition, Whitby, North Yorkshire.

Search and Rescue helicopter, Whitby, North Yorkshire.

Sitting at the harbour, Whitby, North Yorkshire.

Surrounded by seagulls, Whitby, North Yorkshire.

Fortune's Kippers, Whitby, North Yorkshire.

Crabbing, Whitby Harbour, North Yorkshire.

Waiting at the pub, Whitby, North Yorkshire.

Windbreak on the beach, Whitby, North Yorkshire.

Walking through Whitby, North Yorkshire.

Rainy day on the swing bridge, Whitby, North Yorkshire.

Hot dogs, Whitby, North Yorkshire.

Pedestrian waiting area, Whitby, North Yorkshire.

Resting on the Cleveland Way, Robin Hood's Bay, North Yorkshire.

Seagull and feet, Robin Hood's Bay, North Yorkshire.

Walking over wet sand at low tide, Robin Hood's Bay, North Yorkshire.

Round of golf, Ravenscar, North Yorkshire.

Surfers, Hayburn, North Yorkshire.

Sara Whyman walking Tia on the beach, Scarborough, North Yorkshire.

Sitting on the prom, Scarborough, North Yorkshire.

Looking over South Bay, Scarborough, North Yorkshire.

Fishing from sea defences, North Bay, Scarborough, North Yorkshire.

Olympia Leisure, Scarborough, North Yorkshire.

Beach huts, Scarborough, North Yorkshire.

Caravan on the seafront, Scarborough, North Yorkshire.

Backwash wave, Scarborough, North Yorkshire.

Shrove Tuesday Skipping tradition, Scarborough, North Yorkshire.

Fisherman getting ready to leave, Scarborough, North Yorkshire.

Family on the seawall, North Bay, Scarborough, North Yorkshire.

Scarborough mobility, Scarborough, North Yorkshire.

Woman and her dog, beach huts, Scarborough, North Yorkshire.

Sitting on the beach, Scarborough, North Yorkshire.

The harbour, Scarborough, North Yorkshire.

Teddy boy, Scarborough, North Yorkshire.

Foreshore Road, South Bay, Scarborough, North Yorkshire.

Kittiwake, beach huts, Scarborough, North Yorkshire.

Woman on the beach, Scarborough, North Yorkshire.

Mini golf, Filey, North Yorkshire.

Metal detector, Filey, North Yorkshire.

Snoozing on the beach, Filey, North Yorkshire.

Sand boat, Filey, North Yorkshire.

Beach hut, Filey, North Yorkshire.

Café owner, Filey, North Yorkshire.

Sitting in a rock pool, Flamborough, North Yorkshire.

Exploring on the beach, Flamborough, North Yorkshire.

Sitting on the beach, Flamborough, North Yorkshire.

Couple on the beach, Flamborough, North Yorkshire.

Boy running to the beach, Thornwick Bay, Flamborough, North Yorkshire.

Rusty digger, North Landing, Flamborough, North Yorkshire.

Paddling, North Landing, Flamborough, North Yorkshire.

Search and Rescue, Flamborough, North Yorkshire.

Steep climb home, North Landing, Flamborough, North Yorkshire.

Speedboat, Flamborough, North Yorkshire.

Woman and pushchair on sand, Flamborough, North Yorkshire.

Day-trippers, Flamborough, North Yorkshire.

End of the day, North Landing, Flamborough, North Yorkshire.

Couple on rocks at low tide, Flamborough, North Yorkshire.

Young girl with bucket, Flamborough, North Yorkshire.

Dangerous Cliffs, Flamborough, North Yorkshire.

Walking back from the beach, Flamborough, North Yorkshire.

Exploring the rock pools, Flamborough, North Yorkshire.

Couple having a drink, Flamborough Head, North Yorkshire.

Family out walking at Flamborough Head lighthouse, North Yorkshire.

Sitting on the benches at Flamborough Head, North Yorkshire.

Couple next to sculpture, Flamborough Head, North Yorkshire.